The Tempest, an Opera

1756

A FACSIMILE PUBLISHED BY CORNMARKET PRESS
FROM THE COPY IN THE BIRMINGHAM SHAKESPEARE LIBRARY
LONDON
1969

PUBLISHED BY CORNMARKET PRESS LIMITED
42/43 CONDUIT STREET LONDON W1R ONL
PRINTED IN ENGLAND BY FLETCHER AND SON LIMITED NORWICH

SBN 7191 0183 2

THE

TEMPEST.

AN

OPERA.

[Price One Shilling.]

THE
TEMPEST.

AN

OPERA.

TAKEN FROM

SHAKESPEAR.

As it is Performed at the

Theatre-Royal in *Drury-Lane.*

The Songs from Shakespear, Dryden, &c.

The Music composed by Mr. Smith.

LONDON,

Printed for J. and R. Tonson, in the *Strand.*
MDCCLVI.

THE

ARGUMENT.

PROSPERO, Duke of *Milan*, dedicating himſelf entirely to ſtudy, commits the government of his dukedom to his brother *Anthonio*, who, confederating with the king of *Naples*, to extirpate *Proſpero*, they ſeize him and his infant daughter, and force them out to ſea, in a tatter'd boat: Providence drives the boat on ſhore, on a barren inchanted iſland ; where *Proſpero* found nobody but a ſort of incubus ; and here he lives twelve years, in the ſtudy and exerciſe of natural magic. ——At this time the ſame king of *Naples*, *Ferdinand* his only ſon, and *Anthonio*, returning from marrying the daughter of *Naples* to the king of *Tunis*, fall under *Proſpero*'s ſpells.

Here

The ARGUMENT.

Here the OPERA begins.

Prospero, raising a tempest, these princes are cast on shore, and dispersed in this island; the king and *Anthonio* suffer great torments from the supposed loss of the king's son, and from the pangs of their evil deeds: *Ferdinand* is conducted by *Prospero*'s spirits to the sight of *Miranda*, *Prospero*'s daughter; who, till then, had never seen any of mankind except her father. This young pair falling mutually in love with each other, *Prospero* causes the king and his attendants to be brought to his cave; where he owns himself to them. —— And upon this discovery *Anthonio* submits to restore the dukedom of *Milan* to *Prospero* —— and *Miranda* is betroth'd to *Ferdinand*, the king's son.

Dramatis Personæ.

ALONZO, *King of* Naples.

PROSPERO, *The right duke of* Milan.

ANTHONIO, } *His brother, the usurping duke of* Milan.

FERDINAND, *Son to the king of* Naples.

GONZALO, *A nobleman of* Naples.

MIRANDA, *Daughter to* PROSPERO.

CALIBAN, *A savage and deformed slave.*

STEPHANO, *Master of the ship.*

VENTOSO, *Mate.*

TRINCALO, *Boatswain.*

MUSTACHO, *Mariner.*

ARIEL, *An airy spirit.*

Other spirits attending on PROSPERO.

THE

THE
Principal CHARACTERS
Performed by

Mr. B E A R D,

Mr. C H A M N E S S,

Mr. A B I N G T O N,

Mr. R O O K E R,

Mr. G. B U R T O N,

Mr. A T K I N S,

Signora C U R I O N I,

Mrs. V E R N O N,

Miſs Y O U N G, &c.

***

IT is hoped that the Reader will excuſe the omiſſion of many paſſages of the firſt Merit, which are in the Play of the Tempeſt; *it being impoſſible to introduce them in the plan of this Opera.*

THE

THE
TEMPEST.
AN
OPERA.

ACT I. SCENE I.

The Stage darkened --- represents a cloudy sky, a very rocky coast, and a ship on a tempestuous sea. --- ARIEL *comes upon the stage.*

AIR.

RISE, *arise, ye subterranean winds,*
Arise ye deadly blighting fiends ;
Rise you, from whom devouring plagues have birth,
You that i' th' vast and hollow womb of earth
Engender earthquakes, make whole countries shake ;

B   *Ye*

Ye eager winds, whose rapid force can make
All, but the fix'd and solid centre, shake:
Come, drive yon ship to that part of the isle
Where nature never yet did smile.

Myself will fly on board, and on the beak,
In the waste, the deck, in every cabin,
I'll flame amazement. Sometimes I'll divide,
And burn in many places. On the top-maft,
The yards, and bowsprit will I flame diftinctly,
Then meet and join. *Jove*'s lightnings, the precursors
Of dreadful thunder-claps, more momentary
And sight out-running, are the the fire and cracks
Of sulph'rous roaring ; the most mighty *Neptune*
Shall seem to siege, make his bold waves tremble,
Yea, his dread trident shake.   [*Exit.*

Repeated flashes of lightning, and claps of thunder.

SCENE II.

A part of the island near PROSPERO's *cell.*

Enter PROSPERO *and* MIRANDA.

MIRANDA.

If by your art (my deareft father) you have
Put the wild waters in this roar, allay them.
O ! I have suffer'd with those I saw suffer.
Had I been any god of pow'r, I would
Have sunk the sea within the earth, or e'er
It should the goodly ship have swallow'd, and
The freighting souls within her.

A I R.

A I R.

Hark how the winds rush from their caves,
Hark how old ocean frets and raves,
From their deep roots the rocks he tears ;
  Whole deluges lets fly,
  That dash against the sky,
  And seem to drown the stars.

PROSPERO.

Tell your piteous heart, there's no harm done ;
I have done nothing, but in care of thee,
My child, who art ignorant of what thou art ;
But I will now inform thee — pray attend :
'Tis twelve years since thy father was the duke
Of *Milan* —— be not amaz'd, my daughter ;
Thou art a princess of no less issue.

MIRANDA.

O the heav'ns, what foul play had we !

PROSPERO.

Mark me well.
I then neglecting worldly ends, all dedicated
To study, and the bettering of my mind,
Did cast the government on my brother,
Call'd *Anthonio.* — He, from substitution,
And executing the outward face of
Royalty, with all prerogative, did
Believe he was indeed the duke ; hence his
Ambition growing, he confederates

With

With the king of *Naples*, my inveterate foe,
Who, for homage and certain tribute, agrees
To extirpate me from my dukedom, and
To confer fair *Milan* on my brother :
This fettled, and an army levy'd ; one night,
Fated to the purpofe, did *Anthonio* open
The gates of *Milan*, and i' th' dead of darknefs,
The minifters for the purpofe, hurry'd thence
Me, and thy crying felf ; in fine, they forc'd us
Out to fea, in a rotten unrigg'd boat,
Where they left us to the mercy of the winds.

A I R.

In pity, Neptune *fmooths the liquid way,*
Obfequious Tritons *on the furface play,*
And fportful dolphins with a nimble glance,
To the bright fun their glitt'ring fcales advance.
In oozy bed profound the billows fleep,
No clamorous winds awake the filent deep ;
With fafety thro' the fea our boat is bore.
In gentle gales we 're wafted to the fhore.

Here in this ifland we arriv'd, and here
Have I, thy fchool-mafter, made thee more profit
Than other princes can, who have more time
For vainer hours, and tutors not fo careful.

M I R A N D A.

Heav'n thank you for't !

PROS-

PROSPERO.

Know further, that fortune,
Now grown bountiful to this ſhore, hath brought
Mine enemies; and, by my preſcience,
I find my zenith doth depend upon
A moſt propitious ſtar, whoſe influence
If now I court not, but omit, my fortunes
Will ever after drop.——
Thou art inclin'd to ſleep; 'tis a good dulneſs,
And give it way; I know thou can'ſt not chuſe.

A I R.

MIRANDA.

Come, O ſleep, my eyelids cloſe,
Lull my ſoul to ſoft repoſe.

PROSPERO.

Approach, my *Ariel.*

S C E N E III.

Enter ARIEL.

ARIEL.

All hail, great maſter! grave ſir, hail! I come
To anſwer thy beſt pleaſure; be't to fly,
To ſwim, to dive into the fire, to ride

On

On curled clouds ; to thy ftrong bidding task
Ariel, and all his qualities.

A I R.

In the bright moonfhine, while winds whiftle loud,
Tivy, tivy, tivy, we mount and we fly,
All racking along in a downy white cloud:
And left our leap from the sky fhould prove too far,
We flide on the back of a new-falling ftar.
Merry, merry, merry, we fail from the eaft,
Half tippled at a rainbow feaft.

P R O S P E R O.

Spirit, thou haft perform'd to point
The tempeft that I bade thee, and difpos'd
The fhip and princes exactly to thy charge ;
But there's more work : what is the time o' th' day ?

A R I E L.

Paft the mid-feafon.

A I R.

P R O S P E R O.

We muft work, we muft hafte ;
Noontide hour is long fince paft ;
Sprights that glimmer in the fun,
Into fhades already run ;
Naples *will be here anon.*

A R I E L.

ARIEL.

Let me remember thee what thou haſt promis'd.

PROSPERO.

What is't thou can'ft demand?

ARIEL.

My liberty.

PROSPERO.

Before the time be out? No more.
Do'ſt thou forget
The foul witch *Sycorax*, the dam of *Caliban*,
Whom I now keep in ſervice?

ARIEL.

No.

PROSPERO.

Thou do'ſt, and think'ſt it much to tread the ooze
Of the ſalt deep;
To run againſt the ſharp wind of the north,
To do my buſineſs in the veins of the earth,
When it is bak'd with froſt!

ARIEL.

I do not, ſir.

PROSPERO.

Thou beſt know'ſt what torment I found thee in:
It was my art, when I arriv'd and heard thee,
That made the pine, within whoſe rift thou waſt
Impriſoned, to gape and lèt thee out;

And,

And, if thou murmureſt, I will rend an oak,
And peg thee in his knotty entrails, till thou
Haſt howl'd out twelve long winters.

ARIEL.

Pardon, maſter.

PROSPERO.

Go, make thyſelf like a nymph of the ſea;
Be ſubject to no mortal ſight but mine.
Hark thee in thine ear——

ARIEL.

My lord, it ſhall be done.   [*Exit.*

PROSPERO.

Awake, dear heart, awake! Thou haſt ſlept well,
Awake——

MIRANDA.

The ſtrangeneſs of your ſtory put
Heavineſs in me.   [*Exeunt.*

SCENE IV.

Enter FERDINAND—*and* ARIEL *inviſible.*

AIR.

ARIEL.

Come unto the yellow ſands,
And then take hands;

                              Curt'ſy'd

The TEMPEST.

Curt'fy'd when you have, and kifs'd,
The wild waves whift,
Foot it featly here and there,
And fweet fpirits the burthen bear.

FERDINAND.

Where fhould this mufic be, i' th' air, or earth?
It founds no more, and fure it waits upon
Some god of this ifland. Sitting on a bank,
Weeping againft the king my father's wreck,
This mufic hover'd on the waters,
Allaying both their fury and my paffion
With chearing airs: thence I follow'd it,
(Or it has drawn me rather) but 'tis gone;
No, it begins again!

AIR.

ARIEL.

Full fathom five thy father lies;
  Of his bones are coral made :
Thofe are pearls that were his eyes ;
  Nothing of him that doth fade,
But doth fuffer a fea-change,
Into fomething rich and ftrange :
Sea-nymphs hourly ring his knell ;
Hark! now I hear them, ding, dong, bell.

FERDI-

FERDINAND.

This is no mortal bufinefs, nor no found
That the earth owns: I hear it now above me.
It muft mean good or ill, and here I am.

ARIEL.

Here I am.

FERDINAND.

Hah! art thou fo? The fpirit's turn'd an echo.

ARIEL.

An echo.

FERDINAND.

This might feem pleafant, could the burthen of
My griefs accord with any thing but fighs.

ARIEL.

Sighs.

FERDINAND.

And my laft words, like thofe of dying men,
Need no reply.   Fain I would go to fhades,
Where few would wifh to follow me.

ARIEL.

Follow me.

FERDINAND.

I will difcourfe no more with thee,
Nor follow one ftep further.

ARIEL.

One ftep further.

FERDI-

FERDINAND.

This muſt have more importance than an echo.

ARIEL.

An echo.

FERDINAND.

I'll try if it will anſwer when I ſing
My ſorrows to the murmur of this brook.

ARIEL.

This brook.

DUETT.

FERDINAND.

Go thy way.

ARIEL.

Go thy way.

FERDINAND.

Why ſhould'ſt thou ſtay?

ARIEL.

Why ſhould'ſt thou ſtay?

FERDINAND.

Where the winds whiſtle, and where the ſtreams creep,
Under yon willow-tree fain would I ſleep:
    Then let me alone,
    For 'tis time to be gone.

ARIEL.

    For 'tis time to be gone.

There's

> *There's yet in store for thee*
> *Some strange felicity ;*
> *Follow me, follow me,*
> *And thou shalt see.*   [Exeunt.

SCENE V.

Changes to the wild part of the island.

Enter STEPHANO, VENTOSO, *and* MUSTACHO.

VENTOSO.

This will be a doleful day with *Suky.*
She gave me a gilt nutmeg at parting ;
That's loft too. O she's a moft charming wench.

MUSTACHO.

Beshrew thy heart, for thus reminding me
Of my wife : I should ne'er have thought of her ;
But nature will shew itself ; I must melt.

STEPHANO.

Look, look, poor *Mustacho* weeps for grief.

VENTOSO.

In truth, he sheds the brandy from his eyes.

STEPHANO.

Hang wives and miftreffes, let's drink about.

AIR.

A I R.

Here's to thee, Tom, this whining love despise;
Pledge me, my friend, and drink till thou art wise.
It sparkles brighter far than she;
  'Tis pure and right, without deceit;
And such no woman e'er will be;
  No, they are all sophisticate;
Follies they have so numberless in store,
That only he who loves them can have more;
  Neither their sighs nor tears are true,
  Those idly blow, these idly fall;
  Nothing like to ours at all,
    But sighs and tears have sexes too.

Courage, my lads, this island is our own;
The king, the prince, and all their train are drown'd.

V E N T O S O.

Then, my good friends, let's form a government.

S T E P H A N O.

I was the master at sea, and will be
Duke at land: you, *Mustacho,* was my mate,
And now I'm prince, shalt be my viceroy.

M U S T A C H O.

Stephano, let me speak for the people,
Because they are but few, or rather none,
Within this island to speak for themselves:
Know that, to prevent the shedding Christian blood,
  We're

We're content *Ventofo* fhall be viceroy,
Provided I be viceroy over him.
Good people, fay, are ye all fatisfy'd?
What, none anfwer? — Their filence gives confent.

SCENE VI.

Enter TRINCALO *(with a Bottle) half drunk.*

TRINCALO.

I fhall no more to fea;
Here I fhall die on fhore.

VENTOSO.

The ghoft of *Trincalo*, our brave boatfwain!
Be not afraid, 'tis very *Trincalo*.
How got you on fhore?

TRINCALO.

On a butt of fack.
My cellar is a rock, by the fea-fide.

STEPHANO.

Welcome, fubject, to our dominion.

TRINCALO.

What fubject? what dominion? Here, boys,
Here's old fack: I'll be old Simon the king.
But are you all alive? — for *Trincalo*
Will tipple with no ghofts, till he be dead.
Stephano, thy Hand. ———

V E N-

VENTOSO.

You muſt kiſs it then.
He is choſen duke, in full aſſembly.

TRINCALO.

A duke! where? what's he duke of?

MUSTACHO.

This iſland.
Oh, *Trincalo*, we are all made for ever,
The iſland's empty, and all is our own.

VENTOSO.

We two are viceroys o'er all the iſle.

TRINCALO.

What, were matters carried thus againſt me
In my abſence? but I oppoſe it all.

MUSTACHO.

Art thou mad, *Trincalo?* will you diſturb
A ſettled government? where you don't know
The laws of the country?

TRINCALO.

I'll have no laws.

MUSTACHO.

Then civil war begins.

DUETT.

D U E T T.

TRINCALO.

Whilſt blood does flow within theſe veins,
Or any ſpark of life remains,
  My right I will maintain.

MUSTACHO.

Whilſt I this temper'd ſteel can weild,
I'll ne'er to thee, thou braggard, yield;
  Thy threats are all in vain.

TRINCALO.

I defy thee.

MUSTACHO.

I'll not fly thee.

TRINCALO.

Braggard, come.

MUSTACHIO.

——Braggard?
Thy boaſted courage now I'll try;
I ſee thou art afraid to die.

TRINCALO.

Not I.

MUSTACHO.

That's a lye.

TRIN-

TRINCALO.

Lye, Sir?

MUSTACHO.

Ay, Sir.

BOTH.

Behold, I conquer, or I die.

STEPHANO.

Hold, loving fubjects, we'll have no civil
Wars in this our reign; I here appoint
Both you and him my viceroys o'er this ifle.

MUSTACHO *and* TRINCALO.

Agreed.

TRINCALO *fings.*

Then fince no ftate's completely bleft,
Let's learn the bitter to allay,
Infpir'd with this, let's dance and play   [ftriking
  Enjoy at leaft the prefent day,   the bottle.
  And leave to fate the reft.

D   A C T

ACT II. SCENE I.

Another part of the ifland. FERDINAND *dif-covered.*

Enter PROSPERO, MIRANDA, *and* ARIEL.

PROSPERO.

THE fringed curtains of thine eyes advance,
    And fee what is yonder.

MIRANDA.

Is't a fpirit?
Believe me, Sir, it carries a brave form;
But 'tis a fpirit.

PROSPERO.

No; it eats, and fleeps,
And hath fuch fenfes as we, were he not
Somewhat ftain'd with grief (beauties worft canker)
Thou might'ft then call him a goodly perfon.

MIRANDA.

I might call him a thing divine;
Nothing natural I ever faw fo noble.

AIR.

A I R.

FERDINAND.

What sudden blaze of majesty,
What awful innocence of mein,
Is that which I from hence descry?
Like nature's universal queen.

Sure the goddess, on whom these airs attend,
Such beauty cannot belong to human kind.

MIRANDA.

I am like you a mortal, if such you are.

FERDINAND.

My language too! Oh heav'ns! I am the best
Of them, who speak this language, were I but
In my own country. O! if a virgin,
And your affections not gone forth, I'll make you
Queen of Naples.

PROSPERO *sings.*

In tender sighs he silence breaks,
The fair his flame approves,
Consenting blushes warm her cheeks,
She smiles, she yields, she loves.

Young Sir, a word; thou dost here usurp
The name thou ow'st not, and hast put thyself

Upon this ifland, as a fpy to win it
From me, the Lord on't.

FERDINAND.

No, as I am a man.

MIRANDA.

There's nothing ill can dwell in fuch a temple.

PROSPERO.

Speak not you for him ; he's a traitor.   Come,
I'll manacle thy neck and feet together ;
Sea-water fhalt thou drink ; thy food fhall be
The frefh-brook mufcles, wither'd roots, and husks
Wherein the acorn's cradled.—Follow.

FERDINAND.

No:
I will refift fuch entertainment, till
Mine enemy has more pow'r.

> [*He draws, and is charm'd from moving.*

MIRANDA.

O! dear father,
Make not too rafh a trial of him ; for
He's gentle, and not fearful.

AIR.

Sweetnefs, truth, and ev'ry grace,
Which time and ufe are wont to teach,
The eye may in a moment reach,
And read diftinctly in his face.

FERDI.

FERDINAND.

My fpirits, as in a dream, are all bound up:
My father's lofs, the weaknefs which I feel,
The wreck of all my friends, and this man's threats,
To whom I am fubdu'd, are but light to me,
Might I but thro' my prifon, once a day,
Behold this maid! all corners elfe o' th' earth,
Let liberty make ufe of——fpace enough
Have I, in fuch a prifon.

PROSPERO.

Hang not on my garment.

MIRANDA.

Have pity, fir.

PROSPERO.

Speak not for him.   Follow me, fir:
This door fhews you to your lodgings.   [*Exeunt.*

SCENE II.

A wild part of the ifland.

Enter ALONZO, ANTHONIO, *and* GONZALO.

GONZALO.

Befeech you, fir, be merry; you have caufe ·
(So have we all) for joy of our efcape.

ALONZO.

Prithee, peace—My fon is loft.

ANTHO-

ANTHONIO.

Sir, he may live ;
I faw him beat the billows under him,
And ride upon their backs :.
I do not doubt, he came alive to land.

ALONZO.

No, no, he's drown'd.
Thou, *Anthonio*, and myfelf, were thofe
Who caus'd his death.

ANTHONIO.

How cou'd we help it?

ALONZO.

Then, then we fhould have help'd it,
When thou betray'd'ft thy brother *Profpero*,
And his infant daughter, to my power ;
And I, too ambitious, took by force
Another's right——then loft we *Ferdinand* ;
Then brought we thefe fore afflictions on us.

SCENE III.　[*A banquet rifes.*

ARIEL *fings behind the fcenes.*

AIR.

Dry thofe eyes, which are o'erflowing,
All your ftorms are over blowing :
While you in this ifle are biding,
You fhall feaft, without providing ;

Ev'ry

Ev'ry dainty you can think of,
Ev'ry wine which you would drink of,
Shall be your's. All want shall shun you,
Ceres' blessing so is on you.

GONZALO.

See yonder table, set out and furnish'd
With all rarities of meats and fruits!

ALONZO.

But who dares taste this feast?

ANTHONIO.

'Tis certain we must either eat or famish.

ALONZO.

If both resolve, I will adventure too.

SCENE IV. [*The banquet vanishes.*

ARIEL *and the strange shapes appear again.*

AIR.

ARIEL.

Around, around, we pace,
About this cursed place,
While thus we compass in
These mortals and their sin ;
Your vile lives you shall discover,
Truly all your deeds declare,
For about you spirits hover,
That can tell you what they are.

Spirits

Spirits, take them, take them hence,
Make them grieve for each offence.

[The ſpirits dance, and then drive 'em off.

Enter P R O S P E R O.

My charms work ; mine enemies, knit in their
Deſtruction, are now within my pow'r.

A I R.

Upon their broken peace of mind,
　Deſpair, black ſon of guilt, now feeds ;
Whilſt thou, brave youth, in love ſhalt find
　The full reward of virtuous deeds.
No gloſs our guilt can e'er remove ;
　It taints the happieſt day :
But all the pangs of virtuous love,
　Shall virtuous love o'er pay.　　　　[Exit.

S C E N E V.

Before P R O S P E R O's *cell.*

Enter F E R D I N A N D.

To be a priſoner where I love,
Is but a double tie, a link of fortune,
Join'd to the chain of love ; but not to ſee her,
And yet to be ſo near her, there's the hardſhip :
But her fair form lives always in my mind.

A I R.

A I R.

To what my eyes admir'd before,
I add a thousand graces more,
And fancy blows into a flame,
The spark that from her beauty came :
The object thus improv'd by thought,
By my own image I am caught ;
Pygmalion so, with fatal art,
Polish'd the form that stung his heart.

S C E N E VI.

Enter MIRANDA.--PROSPERO, *at a distance, unseen.*

MIRANDA.

Sir, my lord; where are you?

FERDINAND.

Is it your voice, my love ; or do I dream ?

MIRANDA.

Speak softly, it is I.

FERDINAND.

O heavenly creature!
Ten times more gentle than your father's cruel.

MIRANDA.

How do you bear your prison?

E

FERDI-

FERDINAND.

'Tis my palace,
Whilſt you are here.
Admir'd *Miranda*, many a lady
I've ey'd with beſt regard; but you, O you,
So perfect, and ſo peerleſs, are created
Of every creature beſt.

AIR.

In ſome defect each grace was loſt,
  Which touch'd my heart: in thee are join'd
The nobleſt form the earth can boaſt,
  With heavenly innocence of mind.

MIRANDA.

I do not know one of my ſex, nor have I
Seen more men than you, and my dear father;
How features are abroad, I'm ſkilleſs of:
I wiſh not any companion but you;
Nor can imagination form a ſhape,
Beſides yourſelf, to like of.

FERDINAND.

Hear my ſoul ſpeak:
The very inſtant that I ſaw you, did
My heart fly to your ſervice; there reſides,
To make me ſlave to it.

MIRAN-

MIRANDA.

Do you love me?

FERDINAND.

O heav'n! O earth! bear witnefs to this found,
And crown what I profefs with kind event;
Beyond all limit of ought elfe i' th' world,
I do love you.

AIR.

MIRANDA.

How can I fpeak my fecret pain?
  Yet how that fecret pain conceal?
Alas! my filence is in vain!
  My looks my inmoft thoughts reveal.
O, mighty. love! thy power is divine;
  I own its force, and thus my heart refign.

Then hence with bafhful cunning,
And prompt me, plain and holy innocence:
I am your wife, fir, if you approve it.

FERDINAND.

Ay, with a heart fo willing,
As bondage e'er of freedom: here's my hand.

MIRANDA.

And mine with my heart in't: now farewell. [*Exe.*

S C E N E   VII.

Changes to the wild part of the island.

Enter CALIBAN, *with a log of wood upon his shoulders.*

[*A noise of thunder heard.*

C A L I B A N.

All th' infections that the fun fucks up
From bogs, fens, flats, on *Profper* fall, and make him
By inch-meal a difeafe ! His fpirits hear me,
And yet I needs muft curfe.

Enter TRINCALO.

T R I N C A L O.

In the name of wonder, what have we here?
A man, or fifh? for it refembles both:
'Tis fome amphibious monfter of the ifle.
Were I in *England*, as of late I was,
And this monfter to expofe to view,
It would make a man of me for ever :
In *England* any monfter makes a man.
Come hither, monfter.

C A L I B A N.

O torment me not !

TRIN-

TRINCALO.

A fenfible monfter, and fpeaks my language.
Dear tortoife, if thou haft the fenfe of tafte,
Open thy mouth, and know me for thy friend.
                [*Pours the wine down his throat.*

CALIBAN.

A brave god, and bears celeftial liquor.

TRINCALO.

What fay'ft thou, monfter? will you, like me,
Live foberly, and become my fubject?

CALIBAN.

I will fwear to ferve thee.

AIR.

No more dams I'll make for fifh,
    Nor fetch in firing, at requiring,
Nor fcrape trencher, nor wafh difh,
    Ban, Ban, Cacaliban,
    Has got a new mafter; get a new man.

TRINCALO.

Here, kifs the book.   [Caliban *drinks again.*

CALIBAN.

By *Settibos!* this liquor's not earthly;
I pr'ythee, did'ft thou not drop from heaven?

                        TRIN-

TRINCALO.

Only from out the moon, I do assure thee;
I was the man in the moon, when time was.

CALIBAN.

I've seen thee in her, and do adore thee;
My mother shew'd me thee, thy dog, and bush.
Pray be my god, and let me drink again. [*drinks again.*
I'll shew thee ev'ry fertile inch i' th' isle,
Where berries, nuts, and cluster'd filberds grow.

TRINCALO.

Lead there.

CALIBAN.

The distance is too far to reach,
For see, my lord, the night approaches quick.

AIR.

The owl is abroad, the bat, and the toad,
　　And so is the cat-a-mountain;
The ant and the mole sit both in a hole.
　　And frog peeps out of the fountain.

TRINCALO.

Kind monster, stand firm; I see them coming.

CALIBAN.

Whom?

TRINCALO.

The starv'd prince, and his brace of subjects.

Enter

Enter STEPHANO, VENTOSO, *and* MUSTACHO.

CALIBAN.

Thefe fprights fha'n't touch our immortal liquor.

VENTOSO.

Surely he has rais'd the devil to his aid.

MUSTACHO.

Duke *Trincalo*, we have confidered.

TRINCALO.

Say then, is't peace or war?

MUSTACHO.

Peace, and the butt.

STEPHANO.

I come a private perfon now, great duke,
To live content under your government.

TRINCALO.

You fhall enjoy the benefits of peace,
And the firft-fruits, amongft civil nations,
Is to get drunk for joy ; which we'll obferve.
Stephano, thou haft been a falfe rebel ;
Yet I forgive thee : in witnefs whereof
I'll drink foundly.

STEPHANO.

Your grace fhall find, that I
Will do you juftice, and drink as foundly.

TRIN-

TRINCALO.

Drinking is the life of every thing ;
Nothing in nature can subsist without it.

TERZETTO.

TRINCALO.

The thirsty earth soaks up the rain,
And drinks, and gapes for drink again.

STEPHANO.

The plants suck in the earth, and are,
With constant drinking, fresh and fair.

VENTOSO.

The sea itself, which, one would think,
Should have but little need of drink,
Drinks ten thousand rivers up,
So fill'd, that they o'erflow the cup.

TRINCALO.

The busy sun (and one would guess,
By's drunken fiery face, no less)
Drinks up the sea, and when h' as done,
The moon and stars drink up the sun.

ALL.

Earth, seas, sun, moon, and stars do give
Examples how we ought to live.
       [*Trincalo* strikes the bottle after drinking.

A C T

ACT III. SCENE I.

PROSPERO's *cell.*

Enter PROSPERO, FERDINAND, *and* MIRANDA.

PROSPERO.

IF I have too aufterely punifh'd you,
 Your compenfation makes amends ; for I
Have giv'n you here a thread of mine own life,
Or that for which I live. O, *Ferdinand*,
Do not fmile at me, that I boaft her off ;
For thou fhalt find fhe will out-ftrip all praife.

FERDINAND.

I do believe it, againft an oracle.

A I R.

Have you feen but a bright lilly grow,
 Before rude hands have touch'd it ?
Have you mark'd but the fall of the fnow,
 Before the foil hath fmutch'd it ?

F   *Have*

> *Have you felt the wool of the beaver?*
>   *Or ſwan's down ever?*
> *Or have ſmelt o' the bud o' the briar?*
>   *Or the nard i' the fire?*
> *Or have taſted the bag of the bee?*
> *Oh, ſo white! Oh, ſo ſoft! Oh, ſo ſweet is ſhe!*

PROSPERO.

If thou doſt break her virgin-knot before
All ſanctimonious ceremonies may
With full and holy rite be miniſter'd,
No ſweet aſperſions ſhall the heav'ns let fall,
To make this contract grow: therefore take heed,
As *Hymen*'s lamps ſhall light you.

FERDINAND.

Nothing ſhall melt mine honour into luſt,
To ſpoil the edge of that day's celebration.

PROSPERO.

Fairly ſpoken; *Miranda* is thine own.
What *Ariel*; my induſtrious ſervant, *Ariel*——

SCENE

SCENE II.

Enter ARIEL.

ARIEL.

What would my potent mafter? here I am.

PROSPERO.

How fares the king and 's followers?

ARIEL.

Confin'd,
In the fame fafhion as you gave in charge:
The king, his brother, and yours, are all three
Brimful of forrow and difmay; but chiefly
Old *Gonzalo*, his tears run down his beard
Like winter's drops, like ears of reeds; if you
Saw them, your affections would become tender.

PROSPERO.

Haft thou, which art but air, a touch, a feeling
Of their afflictions, and fhall not myfelf,
Paffion'd as they, be kindlier mov'd than thou art?
They being penitent, the fole drift of
My purpofe doth extend not a frown further;
Go, bring them, *Ariel*, hither; and let thy
Meaner fellows fetch the rabble, o'er whom
I gave them pow'r to do it prefently.

AIR.

A I R.

A R I E L.

Before you can say, come and go,
And breathe twice, and cry, so —— so,
Each one tripping on his toe,
Will be here with mop and mow.
Do you love me, master ? ——— No.
   So ready and quick is a spirit of air,
   To pity the lover, and succour the fair,
   That, silent and swift, the little soft god
   Is here with a wish, and is gone with a nod.——

                  [Exit *Ariel.*

S C E N E   III.

P R O S P E R O.

  Look thou be true, and do not give dalliance
Too much the rein : the strongest oaths are straw
To th' fire i' th' blood : be more abstemious,
Or else, good night, your vow.

F E R D I N A N D.

  I warrant you, Sir.
The white, cold virgin-snow upon my heart,
Abates the ardour of my passion.

                    A I R,

A I R.

MIRANDA.

Hope waits upon the flow'ry prime;
   And summer, tho' it be less gay,
Yet is not look'd on as a time
   Of declination, or decay;
For, with a full hand, that does bring
All that was promis'd by the spring.

              [Exeunt *Ferdinand* and *Miranda.*

S C E N E IV.

PROSPERO.

 Now does my project gather to a head,
And little further use have I for charms.
Ye elves of hills, brooks, standing lakes, and groves;
And ye that on the sands, with printless foot,
Do chase the ebbing *Neptune*, and do fly him,
When he comes back ; you demy-puppets, that,
By moon-shine, do the green-four ringlets make,
Whereof the ewe not bites; and you, whose pastime
Is to make midnight mushrooms, that rejoice
To hear the solemn curfew; by whose aid
(Weak masters tho' ye be) I have be-dimm'd
The noon-tide sun, call'd forth the mutinous winds,
                    And

And 'twixt the green fea and the azur'd vault
Set roaring war ; to the dread rattling thunder
Have I given fire, and rifted *Jove*'s ftout oak
With his own bolt—the ftrong-bas'd promontory
Have I made fhake, and by the fpurs pluck'd up
The pine and cedar : graves, at my command,
Have wak'd their fleepers, op'd, and let them forth,
By my fo potent art.   But this rough magic
I here abjure.

A I R.

Let magick founds affright no more,
   While horrors fhake the main ;
Nor fpell-bred ftorms deface the fhore,
   Let facred nature reign !

Deep in the earth, where fun fhall never fhine,
   This cloud-compelling war I place ;
This book th' unfathom'd ocean fhall confine,
   Beyond the reach of mortal race.

S C E N E

S C E N E V.

Enter ARIEL, *followed by* ALONZO, AN-
THONIO *and* GONZALO.

ALONZO.

All torment, trouble, wonder, and amazement,
Inhabits here: fome heav'nly powers guide us
Out of this fearful country————

PROSPERO.

Behold, fir, king,
The wrong'd duke of *Milan, Profpero:*
For more affurance that a living prince
Does now fpeak to thee, I embrace thy body,
And bid thee welcome!

ALONZO.

Be'ft thou he, or no,
Or fome inchanted trifle to abufe,
As late I have been, I know not.   Thy, pulfe
Beats as of flefh and blood ; and, fince I faw thee,
Th' afflictions of my mind amends: this muft crave
(And, if this be all, a moft ftrange ftory)
Thy dukedom I refign, and do intreat
Thou pardon me my wrongs.   But how fhould he
Be living, and be here ?

PROS.

PROSPERO.

You all yet tafte
Some fubtilties o' th' ifle, that will not let you
Believe things certain : welcome, my friends all.
For you, moft wicked fir, whom to call brother,
Would ev'n infect my mouth, I do forgive
Thy rankeft faults.   Know for certain, my friends,
That I am *Profp'ro*, and that very duke
Who was thruft forth of *Milan :*
No more of this ;
For 'tis a chronicle of day by day,
Not fitting our firft meeting.   *Alonzo,*
I'll fhew thee a wonder to content thee
As much as me my dukedom : follow me. [*Exeunt.*

SCENE VI.

Opens to the entrance of PROSPERO's *cell, and difcovers* FERDINAND *and* MIRANDA *playing at chefs.*

MIRANDA.

Sweet lord, you play me falfe.

FERDINAND.

No, my dear love,
I would not for the world.

MIRAN-

MIRANDA.

Yes, for a fcore of kingdoms you fhall wrangle,
And I would call it fair play.

A I R.

FERDINAND.

If on thofe endlefs charms you lay
  The value that's their due,
Kings are themfelves too poor to pay,
  A thoufand worlds too few.
But if a paffion without vice,
  Without difguife or art,
Miranda, *if true love's your price,*
  Behold it in my heart.

S C E N E VII.

Enter PROSPERO, ALONZO, ANTHO-
NIO, GONZALO, *and* ARIEL.

ALONZO.

If this prove
A vifion of the ifland, our dear fon
Shall I twice lofe.

G   FERDI-

F E R D I N A N D.

Though the feas threaten, they are merciful:
I've curfed them without caufe.

[Ferdinand *kneels*.

A L O N Z O.

Now all the bleffings of a glad father
Compafs thee about!

M I R A N D A.

How many goodly creatures are there here?
How beauteous mankind is! O brave new world,
That has fuch people in't.

P R O S P E R O.

'Tis new to thee.

A L O N Z O.

What is this maid with whom thou waft at play?
Your eldeft acquaintance cannot be three hours:
Is fhe the goddefs that hath bro't us hither?

F E R D I N A N D.

Sir, fhe's mortal;
And, O thanks to providence, fhe's mine.
I chofe her when I could not ask my father
For his advice, nor thought I had one.   She

Is

Is daughter to this famous duke of *Milan*,
Of whom I have receiv'd a fecond life.

A I R.

Life refembles April *weather* ;
　　Bright the 'purple dawn appears ;
Noon is fhade and fhine together,
　　Dark the eve defcends in tears.
Follow then the voice of reafon !
　　Ufe the moment as it flies !
Calm in ev'ry cloudy feafon,
　　Gay beneath ferener skies.

ALONZO.

I am her's ;
But oh how oddly will it found, that I
Muft ask my child forgivenefs !

PROSPERO.

There, fir, ftop :
Let us not burthen our remembrance with
An heavinefs that's gone.

ALONZO.

Give me your hands ;
Let grief and forrow ftill embrace his heart
That doth not give you joy.

G 2　　　　　　AIR.

A I R.

PROSPERO *(to* MIRANDA.*)*

With him thy joys shall be compleat,
    Dissolv'd in ease, thy hours shall flow:
With love alone thy heart shall beat,
    And his be all th' alarms you know.
Cares to sooth, and life befriend,
Pleasures on your nod attend.

PROSPERO.

Sir, I invite your highnefs and your train
To my poor cell, where you shall take your rest
For this one night, which (part of it) I'll waste
With such difcourfes, as I doubt not, will make it
Quickly pafs away, and in the morning
I'll bring you to your ship, and so to *Naples* ;
Where I hope to fee the nuptials
Of thefe, our dear beloved, folemniz'd.

ALONZO.

I long to hear the story of your life.

PROS-

PROSPERO.

In proper time, I will deliver all,
And promife you calm feas, aufpicious gales,
And fail fo expeditious, that fhall catch
Your royal fleet far off : my *Ariel*, chick,
This is thy charge, then to the elements,
Be free, and fare you well.

DUETT.

FERDINAND.

Love, gentle love, now fill my breaft,
  The ftorms of life are o'er ;
In thee, my dear Miranda, *bleft,*
  What can I wifh for more.

MIRANDA.

Love, gentle love, and chafte defire,
  My breaft fhall ever move :
Let me thofe heav'nly joys infpire,
  And all our life be love.

FERDI-

FERDINAND.

Thus ever kind,

MIRANDA.

Thus ever true,

FERDINAND.

May I, my sweet one, find,

MIRANDA.

May I be all in you,

Both.

And sacred Hymen *shall dispense*
The sweets of love and innocence.

CHORUS.

Let sacred Hymen *now dispense*
The sweets of love and innocence ;

Let

Let him his choicest blessings shed,
And nobly fruitful be their bed ;
Virtue and love shall deck their crown,
With happy days and high renown.

F I N I S.